D1617560

ADJUSTING
to the
LIGHT

ADJUSTING

to the

LIGHT

Poems by

MILLER WILLIAMS

University of Missouri Press
Columbia and London

University of Missouri Press, Columbia, Missouri 65201
Printed and bound in the United States of America
5 4 3 2 1   96 95 94 93 92

Library of Congress Cataloging-in-Publication Data

Williams, Miller.
  Adjusting to the light : poems / by Miller Williams.
    p.   cm.
  ISBN 0–8262–0851–7 (cloth). — ISBN 0–8262–0852–5 (paper)
  I. Title.
  PS3545.I53352A64   1992
  811'.54—dc20   92–4893
                                                               CIP

∞™ This paper meets the minimum requirements of
the American National Standard for Permanence of Paper
for Printed Library Materials, Z39.48, 1984.

Thanks to the editors of *American Literary Review, Kenyon Review,
Laurel Review, Light, New England Review, New Letters, North Dakota
Quarterly, Puerto del Sol,* and *Southern Review,* in which some of these
poems have appeared. "When I Am Dead, My Dearest" appeared in
The Decade of Dance: A Celebration of Poems, edited by Mark Sanders
(Nebraska: Sandhills Press, 1991). "A Day in the Death" appeared
in *On Doctoring,* edited by Richard Reynolds and John Stone (New
York: Simon and Schuster, 1991).

Designer: Rhonda Miller
Typesetter: Connell-Zeko Type & Graphics
Printer: Thomson-Shore, Inc.
Binder: Thomson-Shore, Inc.
Typeface: Palatino

for Howard Nemerov
Guide to the Ruins

and for Jordan
—how else?

CONTENTS

ADJUSTING
to the
LIGHT

RODIN: *THE CATHEDRAL*
On Coming upon It Unprepared

We had an hour. "—and on the way," she said,
"I want to show you something." A pair of hands
giving empty space a sacred shape,
sacred because a fool understands
a vaulted configuration closing upward.

If hands could dream, they might aspire to this,
to be tense and easy, in charge and groping,
wrapping around a holy nothing. Thus,
the mute might articulate a prayer
with these most human muscles, chosen bones,
by which we came, hand over hand, this far.

Through curving years I have been sustained by stones,
David, the *Pietà*. Now, two more hands.

"Are you all right?" she said. "We have to leave."

"It's strange," I said. "At first it made me happy
and then it made me sad." She said, "Like love?"

More than love, this trickery of light,
a frozen mathematics of the eye,
a wedding of love and logic we call art,
a dark we see and the light we see it by.

Beauty is in the marriage. Our delight
is in the prospect. The lagging sadness lies
in living to know that though it is made of us
we never can quite see what it signifies.

DURING A FUNERAL SERVICE
THE MIND OF THE YOUNG PREACHER
WANDERS AGAIN

"We come," he says, "to bury an empty shell."
Which is true and says nothing. He thinks of this.
He thinks of Hume. So far as he can tell
nobody sees the small parenthesis

enclosing his head, although the old phrases
which are his obligation continue to pour
out of his mouth. He lifts his eyes and gazes
past the congregation, past the shore

on which, he tells them, all the believing dead
are waiting for us always. He shuts his eyes.
He is unaccountably tired. He bows his head,
in which a thought is worming its way. He tries

to concentrate on saying what ought to be said
to people undone as one from this man,
that he is not gone for good, but gone ahead.
It's happened before. He does the best he can,

though times like this—it is a growing peace—
he half suspects the dead don't ever look
our way again, once gone from this blue space,
don't have the wherewithal for looking back,
and have no truck, if he knows the simple truth,
with any trick we fall for, not life, not death.

ADJUSTING TO THE LIGHT

—air—air! I can barely breathe . . . aah!
Whatever it was, I think I shook it off.
Except my head hurts and I stink. Except
what is this place and what am I doing here?

Brother, you're in a tomb. You were dead four days.
Jesus came and made you alive again.

Lazarus, listen, we have things to tell you.
We killed the sheep you meant to take to market.
We couldn't keep the old dog, either.
He minded you. The rest of us he barked at.
Rebecca, who cried two days, has given her hand
to the sandalmaker's son. Please understand
we didn't know that Jesus could do this.

We're glad you're back. But give us time to think.
Imagine our surprise to have you—well,
not well, but weller. I'm sorry, but you do stink.
Everyone, give us some air. We want to say
we're sorry for all of that. And one thing more.
We threw away the lyre. But listen, we'll pay
whatever the sheep was worth. The dog, too.
And put your room the way it was before.

A DAY IN THE DEATH

He is amazed how hard it is to die.
He lies in the hospital bed, his shallow breaths
audible in the hall. He wonders why—
and tries to laugh because he knows—the deaths
of heroes always seem to be so quick.
Because, he knows, heroes have to fight,
and die fighting; also they rarely get sick.
A nurse looks into the room to say good night.
They don't tell each other what they know,
that both hope these words are the last he'll hear,
but guess they aren't. He thinks of the undertow
all swimmers swimming in strange waters fear,
that grabs you from below. He tries to sink
deep enough beneath the surface of sleep
to be found there and lost. There is a stink
thickening in the room. He knows the cheap
perfume Death wears. Why does she stand around?
Why doesn't the bitch take him? He tries to laugh
and this time does, and jerks at the new sound.
Well, half is already gone; the other half
could be a survivor of Buchenwald. Today
a counselor held his hand and told him again
to let go, to let it slip away.
He turned back to see how long it had been
since he had held on. He almost said,
"I'm trying. Something's stuck. Give me a shove."
He almost did. He squeezed the hand instead,
once for reasons forgotten and once for love.
But now he tries to sleep, pretends he is led
down through a wandering tunnel, sweetly gray,
to join the deep society of the dead,
afraid when the sun comes they'll send him away,
back to that room, back to that shrinking bed,
to lie there, being a lie, another day,
his eyes, his enormous eyes, eating his head.

4

ON NOT WRITING A LOVE POEM

How do I say
what everybody says
as if it hasn't been said
by everyone?

What can I do
(considering all the dead)
that isn't banal, pretending
it hasn't been done?

There is no death,
love, birth, that isn't trite.
If all our passions are long-
discovered islands

patterned with footprints,
a Sunday tourist sight,
let people (cupping their ears)
say, "Listen: what silence."

EXCUSE ME

Give me just a second before you start.
Let's agree on what you're reading here.
Let's call it a poem, a poem being an act
of language meant to hold its own exceptions,
which you therefore read with a double mind,
accepting and rejecting what you find.

If part of what you find is what you brought,
let's call this reading a poem, one of the games
imaginations play when they meet.
If you suspect you may not have the wit
to face the other player, one to one,
then you can be a deconstructionist
and make believe the other doesn't exist,
though that will be like sitting on one end
of a seesaw in summer, wishing you had a friend.

TO A FRIEND, AN UNHAPPY POET

You fret how few now read what's hard to write.
There barely are any
but this is not something we can fix.
There never were many.

About the same percentage of people always
could love a noun.
What mother in London's slums opened her Blake
or Milton after the children were yelled down?

More to the point, how many quoting stocks
could quote Carew?
How many people in Mansfield Park read Austen?
The question was never how many but why and who.

Because millions can say the printed word
you think they should read
not signs and menus and scores and labels but us.
They know what they need.

A SHORT HISTORY OF THE GAME

A century taking its turn
at the crest of the curve of time
sees in itself entertainers
who work its arenas and stages,
but actors and athletes and singers
deserve neither credit nor blame
for how human beings behave.
They didn't devise the game.

A century looking down
the long curve to the past
sees mathematicians and poets
but mathematicians and poets
deserve neither credit nor blame
for how human beings behave.
They didn't devise the game.

Acclaim while you live is a thing
they give you for being forgotten
increasingly after you're dead.
Esteem after death is quiet
but faithful in the bed.

THE DEATH OF CHET BAKER

Somewhere between *Amazing Grace*
and *Great Balls of Fire* we heard
the horn first and then the voice
like Billie Holiday's. Old Bird,

he knew a secret. So did Diz.
But Chet, he struck him up a deal
with dark angels. Angel he was
and dark he was. Truth to tell,

he darkened till he fell away
wearing twice his fitting years,
still playing at what he had to say,
sometimes putting on some airs

but they were his. He put them on
like pants and shoes, a wrinkled shirt.
What do we feel, now that he's gone?
What of the hollow? How does it hurt?

Hotly as shame? Sharply as scorn?
As dimly as an old rebuke?
There was a hophead with a horn
who stopped a concert to puke,

who couldn't read the notes he played,
who couldn't love a person long,
who blew the breath of souls afraid
into muted, seamless song.

But what to pity these pitiless days?
He had his dreams and methadone,
we have tapes and CDs,
Time after Time, When Your Lover Has Gone.

CDs do what was done before
over and over and over and over,
never adding a note more
if we should listen to them forever.

Wherever we are he isn't there.
Love him. Love him in the loss
for all the things he did with air.
The Thrill Is Gone. Poor Chet. Poor us.

     Epitaph
Once a Jazzman, playing high,
raised up his horn and tried to fly.
He got above the oxygen
and fell back to earth again.
The body here beneath this stone
was Chet Baker, who has flown.

THINGS
J.C., 1916–1986

The day we went to visit the house of the poet
I sat in the chair he sat in when he died
to look at the last things he looked at:
the cribbage board; the blue wall; the clock,
the slow brass pendulum; the deck of cards;
the small Picasso, slapdash black on white,
almost oriental, one foot by two;
the black round telephone with the circular dial;
the rug with wine roses; books on the floor.
I sat until the pendulum took my attention
to feel what he might have felt, sitting there.

For nothing, of course, for all my foolishness.
The dying gave the room its brown meaning.
When he sat down, the chair was just a chair.

DURING THE HYMN BEFORE THE CHRISTMAS SERMON THE MIND OF THE YOUNG PREACHER WANDERS AGAIN

'For God to send a son into the world
meant, in fact, for Him to give His son
into the realm of time. But how could the two
speak with each other, then? *Thy will be done,*

orders, supplications, the sound waves
built on passing time, though it doesn't pass
inside the mind of God. He must hear nothing,
at rest in an infinite never. An always. I guess.

What do I know about space and time?
Almost nothing. I ought to hide my face,
sitting here hoping to know God,
whose simplest thought may be time and space.

But how would He think, time being nothing to Him?
There's a puzzle for you. I would think thought
means process of a sort, and process, time,
though I have only the math that I was taught.

The fact is we have little enough to work with
in coming to see what might make any sense
inside the mind, whatever it is, of God.
What we call acts and scientists call events

are equally beyond us. We are like fruit
hungering to understand the tree.'
He likes it but he doesn't have the time
to lean back and enjoy the simile.

The closing chords have moved him to his feet.
The people sit and wait. He looks at them
so long they start to look at one another.
"In Judea," he says, "in Bethlehem . . ."

MORNING AT THE ZAGORSK MONASTERY OUTSIDE MOSCOW

She bent so low
she bruised her gnarly knuckles against the ground.
She was so slow
she could barely keep even with her cane.
She was so old
she may not have remembered having teeth.
When she was told
the monastery was closed for the weekend
she was so sad
her tiny face screwed itself together.
She lived, she said,
through the revolution, the civil war,
the stormblast
when Germany laid siege to Leningrad.
She meant to last
a few more years, so she could go to heaven
when everyone went,
with the last sunset of the second thousand years.
The last event.
That way she wouldn't have to go alone.
They said, she said,
we did not need to come here anymore,
Christ being dead,
killed in our streets in 1917.
What does that say?
Everybody we'll see in heaven is dead.
One blinding day
we'll all go up before him, begging grace.
I am so old,
she said, that children cannot count that far.
I've never told
anybody all the things I know.
I say a prayer
for poor Joseph Stalin, for all those years

when he was there
in every mirror, in every telephone.
He comes in dreams,
bloody and torn, dripping with remorse,
or so it seems.
Who knows what is actual on this earth?
Nevertheless,
what it comes to, poor God being dead,
is saying yes.
That is what I say. It's what I've said
these awful years.
I don't see any point at all now
in spending tears
on those that haven't said it. Let them lie.
I almost grieved
once for old Stalin, who I suppose
truly believed
there wasn't any God, and now he knows.

ARCHITECTURE OF THE AMERICAN MIND

It happened, halfway through the nineteen hundreds,
that all things old and ugly were abhorrent.
The past, like unwanted knowledge, embarrassed people.
Buildings of red clay bricks on town squares
all over the country were given aluminum skin.

"We have a past," we said, "in our own way.
You'll see no sign of it here, look as you may."

During the century's closing years, the past,
working out from cornices and cracks,
was loved again, and many dollars were spent
to pull the skins away from the warm bricks.
Nobody recalled the strange embarrassment.

"We have a past," we said, "a yesterday
long, drab, and odd. Like London, you might say."

THE SIX MORAL VIRTUES
Grace, Style, Class, Humility, Kindness, and Wisdom

Not to glance at anyone else, looking full in the face
at someone telling a story a third time—this is grace.

Letting the crabby driver hold his hand a long while
before you drip a small tip coin by coin—this is style.

Ignoring knowing eyes, the grin behind the lifted glass,
as if there were no secrets to be known—this is class.

To die with everyone you know let loose from promises
with no small cry to call them after you, faint SOS,

but going in a style for those you leave to fumble toward
when you won't know, is style with class and grace, a closing
   chord.

I think if we had stopped to point them out, to say, You show
these somethings, What do you call them? You would have said, I
   don't know.

That's four of six. If you were somewhat kind, a little wise . . .
Here you would have said, now don't go getting into lies.

But I was there and am a witness here and I can swear
you carried them as quietly as the virus, and as unaware.

PULLING BACK

Here in my drive in the rain,
a bright, little sprinkle of rain,
with the wipers turned off, I can see
a Monet of my house and my lawn,
and I wonder why anyone cares
what a newspaper editor thinks
or if Dan'l Boone kilt a bear
or if one day the sun will burn out
or what seven-year-olds want to wear.

WHEN I AM DEAD, MY DEAREST

Sing what you want to sing. Theologize.
Let anyone who wants to lie tell lies.
What will I care, back in the past tense
with no ambition and not a gram of sense,
back where I was before a fear and a wish
joined to form a sort of finless fish
that learned to walk and have lips and smile?
I will go there to wait an endless while,
and neither think that wrong nor wish it right,
more than a rock in darkness hopes for light.
You will say my name, but less with years,
the children less than you and more than theirs.
It's mostly in our names, as they fray and thin,
blown on the breaths of aging friends and kin,
that in some tugging moments we may seem
to sleep on a little past the dream.

COPING

So let us suppose that after everybody
goes to bed or shift-work Monday night,
filled with sweet contingencies and regrets,
they wake or go home astonished at Wednesday morning.
Some might call in their debts, some pay their debts.
Others might argue whether a missing day
meant one day more or one day less to live.
Some would knock with warnings, door to door.
Some would do what they had planned for Tuesday
and never think about it anymore.

HELLO. I'LL BET YOU DON'T KNOW WHO THIS IS.

A friend has come by after twenty years
and I am older than before he came.
The nervous socialist no longer stirs
behind the rimless glasses. Besides his name,

the voice, the glasses, hardly anything
is what he was. Can it have been so long?
He sits with his wife as we trade remembering
and looks at me as if I remember wrong.

Despairing of understanding
We fall into decadence

Though all our innocence cannot console us
for what we don't know, sometimes even so,
there's pleasure in it. Full of ignorance

we lie on the living room rug empty as lizards.
By waning dinner candles and two small lamps
we kiss and read all night, Wyatt and Welty,

and others who taught us the world, who taught us time,
and change, the always faster breathing of time,
and the flickering possibilities of words.

Along its cold descent of days and nights
the tumbling earth turns us toward the sun
to send us to bed. Fumbling and out of phase

with the first stirring birds and yawning beasts
and countless imperceptibly shifting leaves,
we rouse ourselves past noon, with no chores done.

Icu: SPACE/TIME IN THE WAITING ROOM

There faded from her features what was her.
She could have been her sister. A day or two,
She could have been a cousin. A couple more,
she might have been someone I never knew.

She was so far off and set on going,
I couldn't make her hear me yesterday.
She got smaller and smaller. Now this morning,
I think she could be coming back this way.

I CAN ONLY STAY FOR FIFTEEN MINUTES

"Oh," the doctor mumbled, "she's doing as well
as anyone could expect." He's said it before.
Still you lie here shrinking, cell by cell,
as if you don't understand what a deathbed's for.

If there is someone there at last to tell,
say that we want out easier. Say that we fear,
more than the face of God or faces of hell,
dying before we die. Say we'd prefer

not spending nine more months finding our way
back out of the world. The mind knows well enough.
It's this mule of a body that wants to stay,
forgetting and fussing till everything falls off.

The old gods might listen. They used to play
with all the fine distinctions: dignity, shame,
hubris, cowardice, watching night and day.
If they are out there still, they might still dream

of getting involved again. Tell them you came
one of the hard ways and how we can miss
deciding things for ourselves. Give them my name,
who comes up next and doesn't need any of this—
the little smell, the patience, the awful blame.

CLOSING THE HOUSE

That's never going to fit inside the box.
They took the picture to help them do her hair.
I guess we just throw out the underwear
but what are we to do with all the books?
Praise Him, honey, she's gone to where He's at.
Love goes to love for all the love we miss.
Who can tell me what to do with this?
I think Aunt Agnes always wanted that.

WALKING AFTER SUPPER
for Howard

It is when I have thought of the universe
expanding until an atom becomes the size
of a solar system and millions of years pass
during the forming of a single thought,
of some place where gigantic young are taught
that we were here (though this will be known
by no evidence but logic alone,
all signs of us, and even our sun, gone),

that I have sometimes had to remind myself
that, say, if in a car at a crosswalk
a woman waves for me to go ahead,
this act deserves attention; that her doing that
equals in gravity all that has ever been
or will have been when we and the sun are dead.
All this I think in Fayetteville, Arkansas,
frozen here on the curb, in love, in awe.

LEARNING RUSSIAN

First the elaborate letters, then their sounds,
the fat, embarrassed tongue feeling its way,
and then the words, heavy with consonants,
tied uselessly together for something to say
to him that meets me mornings in the mirror,
both of us dour, both of us Muscovites:
I want to buy four refrigerators.

Learning the long winter, the snow-blue lights.
Then getting used to leaving small words out:
My mother old; I go work, good-bye.

Becoming romantic, the hand against the brow,
and then learning to build the occasional lie
I've learned to live with in my own language.
They work as well; we are what we are.

Then talking about the government in whispers,
loving the Winter Palace, hating the czar.

THE GROOM KISSES THE BRIDE
AND THE MIND OF THE YOUNG PREACHER
WANDERS AGAIN

He knows what it signifies, lifting the veil,
but wonders where it started—the Gauls, the Huns,
maybe, he thinks, the Druids. Likely the Druids.
Say a thousand years, and the smelly beginnings.
Back to the shaman, singing the words of wedding
from Old High German *wager,* Old Norse *pledge.*
Back to the husband, Old Frisian, *house,* and *bondage.*
Back to the wife, of unknown origin.
Back to the circle of elders, closing and watching,
back to the careful lifting of the dress,
down to the bearskin rug, the body surprised,
until the lute signals the celebration
meaning another member of the tribe
might have been begun. How would that be,
he wonders, being one of such a circle,
unmoving, unmoved as the gray circling stones.
Or would they applaud? Why would they not applaud?

The laughing music from *Lohengrin* takes her away.
They will be children, he thinks, for a little while,
flesh upon flesh on the bed or the front room floor,
then they may learn to listen to slower songs.
Naked she would speak of the glory of God
and God be with you always, go in peace,
but everyone is gone, the organist, even,
has folded up her music and gone home.

27

Rubrics

GLASNOST: MOSCOW, THE ARBAT

"There is much to fear," she said. "We fear
we'll flap our wings and fall."
"But now there is hope," I said. She said,
"We fear that most of all."

ON HEARING SOME BLACK STUDENTS FLIP EPITHETS AT ASIAN STUDENTS TRYING TO THROW A FOOTBALL

Is this a progress to embrace,
that these have found this widening place
in what we call the mainstream
of what we call the American dream?

SIX O'CLOCK, THE AIRPORT IN ATHENS

A traveler spreads a paper, removes his shoes,
bows, kneels, and touches his forehead to the floor,
lifts his head and touches it down again.
Another catches it on his camcord.
Some do what they must, some what they can.

MISE EN SCÈNE

So his friends will think him smart
he grabs a chance to use words like *athwart,*
durst, epistaxis, dour, and *thence.*
He turns them lightly, given half a chance.

Chances are few, but now and then
he seems the most erudite of men.
Or so he thinks. Friends, I'm afraid,
think him gauche and largely gasconade.

RUNNING OUT OF ANYTHING TO SAY
Last Lines for L., Who Was Stiff before He Had to Be

He scorned to have a mucous membrane
or gas or socks unmatched and would have hated
to have this single eulogizing quatrain
truncated.

HOME FROM THE GRAVE TO NEWS OF WAR AND MADNESS

There may be no sign of divinity in us—
those human hungers we call love aside—
but that unnamed and disconcerting need
that stirs afresh when one of us had died.

A POEM FOR FLANNERY BUT NOT THE ONE I PROMISED

I stay your loving failure, not by choice.
I promised I would do it and I will.
Every time I've started, though, a voice
has said *not yet, not yet* and does still.

FLESH

Discolored by mold and fungus, rotting wood
is always a beautiful and sweet-smelling thing.
All rotting flesh is abhorrent to the senses,
so kneeling down we pray and rising sing
for fabled mercy of a possible God. And we should.

IN MEDIAS RES

Each of us stares, an astonished I,
from the center of all. This may be only
how it seems or may be why
we feel, till dark by dark we die,
like Gods, important and lonely.

ON SEEING A PHOTOGRAPH BY MATTHEW BRADY

In 1863 whole towns
carried lunches to hillsides
to watch a war. Some made bets.
Some tried to recognize their kin.
Now my wife and I take meals
watching several worlds away
a war too big for battlefields,
a war too far for us to say
which are kin. All could as well
be kin for all that we can tell.

THE DEAD IN WAR
for T. H.

We name their rigid names in books and prayer
and see in dreams and movies how they died
and set a place and day for them aside
and live without the lives they magnified.
This doesn't mean they know that we forebear
or, if they know, it doesn't mean they care.

SUM, ES, EST

Each of us stands dead center on a stage
but in the wings of someone else's play,
everyone the uncontested star,
everyone the ill-tonsured stooge,
and all the roles between. How can we say
who someone is but in the play we are?

THE STRIPPER

You're too young for this. I was twenty.
What are you? Eighteen, maybe? Seventeen?
You know the cops are going to check your papers.
What do they call you? Jean? They call you Jean?
That won't do. That won't do at all.
We'll need to find something sort of, well,
you know, a name nobody ever had.

You sure you want to do this? I wouldn't tell
no one I know to work here, a hundred men
yelling things to you about your tits,
you don't really feel complimented.
If I had a place to go, I'd call it quits
so quick you could put your hand in the hole
where I used to be. But when you're down,
I don't know, it makes you feel good
to be admired by a man from some town
where no one ever saw a woman naked
with all the lights turned on, married or not.
I figure I might have stopped a few divorces
by just relieving the pressure somewhat.

I assume Jean is your real name.
So keep it. I was told to teach you how
to move about and take your clothes off.
I guess you figure you can do that now,
except for being so bashful you can't talk.
Well, you don't have to talk. Just be sincere.
That's the whole secret, so everyone
can make believe that no one else is here.
Lord, look at you, honey. I bet you've got
half a Greyhound ticket still in your purse.

Pretty soon you won't know yourself.
You won't even want to. What's worse,
not many others are going to know you, either.
Not men, I mean. Not in a happy way.
Every man wants his woman a secret.
Except in swimming. Swimming, the bitch can lay
her body down where everybody sees,
with nothing but her crotch and nipples hid.
You can't do that for cash and be a lady.
Though Gypsy Rose Lee was and did.
Once in a while somebody beats the odds.

I'm supposed to show you how to hunch.
The first thing is, not to be so fearful.
Shake it up a little. That buys your lunch.
It won't be you up here. You'll be a hundred
nights that used to be or might have been.

And smile at all the women. Some are here
to see what you have to show them, same as the men.

So, anyway. You got to have your props.
I use a chaste lounge and a telephone.
Use a wooden horse if you want to.
The only thing, you got to be alone.
Don't share the stage with anybody ever.
Scores every night are going to climb up here
in their imaginations. That's crowd enough.

You have to throw out a souvenir,
something cheap that you can buy a box of.
First they'll have the comic out there
relaxing everybody except you.
You'll be back there wondering what to wear.

You know they've brought you in to put me out.
I kind of thought they might be going to.
What can you do? You give them all you've got.
I don't know. I guess I take a few
too many now and then. I got some veins
you don't have to look too close to see.
It seems like every day I hang looser.
I look in the mirror, I can't believe it's me.

Anyway, start out with what you're wearing.
Button up your blouse all the way.
You have to begin with everything proper.
You'll probably end up wearing a negligee
that you can see through, but first of all,
you come in from a date. You close the door.
You pick his picture up and look at it.
You let your blouse and skirt fall to the floor.
Then your slip. You have to have a slip.
And then your bra first and then your pants.
Keep your stockings on. Real stockings.
Move slow. Slow. To music. Like a dance.

You're pretty as anything I ever saw.
Let me ask you something. What would you do
if one of your family wandered in here?

Your daddy, say, but didn't know it was you,
the smoke and colored lights? Now touch your breast
like this to show you're feeling succulent.
You need to have your lips a little surprised,
your fingers playing the air like an instrument.

There's this little place where I like to go.
They have good boiled shrimp and a nice bar.
We've done enough for now. I'd like to know
where you stood in your graduating class,
what magazines you read, if you like to sew,
and who in a hundred hells you think you are.

OUT OF A CLEAR SKY

You've wanted to hear my voice, so hear me now.
I know it must have seemed a long time.
You have to know I've carried you as a thought.
You're every one my creatures and I love you,
going about your wars and ball games.

You think I don't give my attention to games?
There is nothing, you might say, beneath me.
Though seen in another way, everything is.

Everything between us is paradox.
You've said you want to be the way I want you.
I have wanted to be whatever you wanted
whenever you called my name, whatever it was.
For some, a face with brief and human emotions.
For some, only a love that knows its name.
My name is, well, the cause of everything.

Some ask, If I created space and time,
where did I exist before I did it?
None of this is your concern at all.
All you have to know is, I am here.

Recall the lonely feeling when you doubt me.
Though when this occurs it's mostly my fault.
I could have had you smarter than you are.
Still, may I be praised, you are my thoughts.
I called it good. I still call it good.

I'm talking here. Is anybody listening?
Why aren't you on the rooftops, into the streets?
What do you think you're hearing here, thunder?

I'm not asking that to get an answer.
You know I know the answer before I ask.
It's just a way of moving a question forward,
like "Where is your brother?" Like "Who said you were naked?"
Like "How would you like to see the world on fire?"

That's just to scare you. I still hold the thought
wrapped in the thought I had of everything
flying away from me, with little clots
collecting here and there and having thoughts.

You are the sweetest, most chaotic thought
of all these thoughts that fly forth, making time.
I'll hold it till it all comes back to me.

And in the meantime, listen when I talk.
Why do you think I thought you in the beginning?

FOLDING HIS *USA TODAY*
HE MAKES HIS POINT IN THE BLUE STAR CAFE

There's this bird I saw in the paper, they said
was a long time on that endangered list
but isn't now because they're all dead.
It didn't have a place to put its nest.
So what we're out is, we're out a bird.
It never weighed an ounce, and what I read,
the thing was hardly seen or even heard
by much of anyone. So now it's spread
across a half a page. Do-gooders, they'll
undo us yet. If it was, say, a deer,
that did some good. Or bass. OK. Or quail.
We are talking about a sparrow here.
Maybe there's something I don't understand.
Anyone's cooked a sparrow, raise your hand.

THE SHRINKING LONESOME SESTINA

Somewhere in everyone's head something points toward home,
a dashboard's floating compass, turning all the time
to keep from turning. It doesn't matter how we come
to be wherever we are, someplace where nothing goes
the way it went once, where nothing holds fast
to where it belongs, or what you've risen or fallen to.

What the bubble always points to,
whether we notice it or not, is home.
It may be true that if you move fast
everything fades away, that given time
and noise enough, every memory goes
into the blackness, and if new ones come—

small, mole-like memories that come
to live in the furry dark—they, too,
curl up and die. But Carol goes
to high school now. John works at home
what days he can to spend some time
with Sue and the kids. He drives too fast.

Ellen won't eat her breakfast.
Your sister was going to come
but didn't have the time.
Some mornings at one or two
or three I want you home
a lot, but then it goes.

It all goes.
Hold on fast
to thoughts of home
when they come.
They're going to
less with time.

Time
goes
too
fast.
Come
home.

Forgive me that. One time it wasn't fast.
A myth goes that when the quick years come
then you will, too. Me, I'll still be home.

SHE PRAYS FOR HER HUSBAND, THE GOOD PASTOR LYING ON HIS DEATHBED AT LAST

He wants to go somewhere he hasn't been.
He's tired of where he's been. He wants to go
away from here, away from earth, from dirt.
He's tired of everything that humans know.
He longs to know what no one ever knew:
invisible shapes, a love without a name,
women and men who go about their being
without praise, ambivalence, or blame.
Hormones and hope and five-dollar perfume
take us places he has not been to much,
make us tell old lies to one another,
bore each other to sleep, and darkly touch.
Letters to newspapers, and bad sermons,
these were his major sins, his joy these.
Take his soul home and make it feel at home,
filled with the love of you and ill at ease.

THE SERIAL MURDERER SAYS SOMETHING TO THE PRIEST

If we all go, seeing we all were made
from nothing, to nothing again, I'm ready to go.
But if there is a place for beings to be
after we thought we had it out of the way,
someplace I might be met by shade after shade
of them that died in my hands, well, I confess,
that I would be uneasy. I'd be afraid.
But then I guess I'd naturally go to hell
and they'd be elsewhere, mostly. Truth to tell,
I'd rather be damned alone than have them wait,
watching for me to come to where they are,
hovering, silent, dark with knowledge and hate.
Still I'd rather face them again than forget
their grand, identical eyes, begging and wet.

THE HEAD OF THE WANDERING FAMILY SPEAKS OF HIS BROTHER

He didn't have to use that tone of voice,
not with the kids and not with you, either.
Whatever else, I am his only brother.
You are my wife and these here are my boys.

He had no right. But still I understand
he has a lot of things to worry about.
We had the same chance starting out,
then, I don't know, things got out of hand.

When I said he wasn't quite as good
as what he thought, I sounded like a snob
the same as him. I guess we ought to call—

considering he told us that we would,
what with the kids and still no kind of job,
what with winter coming on and all.

THE ART PHOTOGRAPHER PUTS HIS MODEL AT EASE

Well, good. You got here. Let me take your things.
I hope it wasn't hard to find your way.
Have a seat by the window. A new model,
I like to talk a while and get to know her.
It lets us relax. I do mean both of us.
Truth to tell, I'm a pretty shy person.
Of course I have to get around that.
Maybe you'd like some tea. A diet drink?
You're not from here, right? I envy you that.

I was twelve before I knew the sky
was any other color but charcoal gray.
That's why light matters to me so much.
Light and dark, the way they play together.
Chiaroscuro is what the Italians call it.

I hope you remembered about the underwear.
The lines from all the elastic and the straps
can take an hour or two to go away.
You're on the clock from when you closed the door.
I can't pay you to sit around and wait
for bra and panty impressions to smooth out.
It's just a practical thing, you understand.

But it's all right. There isn't any hurry.
A couple of minutes now, relaxing a little,
it's going to save me more than what it cost
once we go inside and get to work.

I know you feel nervous, not wearing any.
Well, but that's not quite the problem is it?
More my knowing you don't have any on.
You'll get used to that. After a while
you won't even think about it. I certainly don't.

I hate to see it happen, to tell the truth.
There's something about a model the first time,
something—what can I call it? Modesty, maybe?—
that says you're not used to being looked at,
not used to having someone see so much,
not every crevice and curve. There's a sweetness
in such an innocence. A mystery, too,
and I might say a sadness, that gets lost later.

So how do you pout? Let me see you pout.
You don't have to purse the lips so much.
Pretend that you're about to say *please*
just with the last sniffle after you've cried.
How would you like a little glass of wine?
Sometimes it helps. It brings a light to the face.

I guess you're nervous now about getting undressed.
You don't have to do it in front of me.
You get behind a screen. There's a camisole there,
so you don't come out with nothing on.
Models don't walk around with nothing on.
The naked body walking around is erotic.
We have to be careful about that.
It is an intimate relationship,
model and artist, artist and model. It can be.
I could tell you some that were great lovers.
Models have killed themselves because of this.
All that attention, every curve and crevice
making the brush make every curve again.
Hell, no wonder.

                    Let me pour you some wine.
You'll find the studio chilly. I keep it that way.
It tightens the skin and brings the nipples out.

Look at the time. Where did the time go?
Go on and finish your wine. We want to be sure
you're feeling at ease in every part of your body.
I can't work with a self-conscious model.
If you're embarrassed others will be embarrassed.

I can tell you hadn't thought of that,
about how many people are going to see you.
You could be famous, you know. Some models are famous.
I'm glad you answered the ad. You'll be fine.
I knew on the telephone you'd be fine.

You're also going to make a little money.
Which of course is what you're doing here.
What else? It's not for art. Hell, me neither.
I mean, I do it because I have a compulsion.
No artist creates art because it's art.
An artist makes what people may call art
because, whatever you call it, it has to be done.
You must be needing money pretty badly.

You truly are a very lovely woman.
Barely a woman, right? Show me the pout.
Now sit up straight and hold your shoulders back.
Your breasts are set high and they hold to the center
and seem almost more conical than round.
That's good. It means that when you lie down
they won't slide off your chest like fried eggs.

Now when we get inside, forget I'm here.
Get undressed and walk straight to the couch.
Breathe deeply. Let the camisole float to the floor.
Pretend you're waiting naked for a lover.
All art is pretend. You just forget I'm here.
If you can't do that, why don't you make believe
I'm watching you from a window across the street.
You just sit and think about your lover.
Then lie down. OK. I think we're ready.

HELLO

Whoever you are, you have the number you dialed.
We probably could but will not come to the phone.
We can talk on the other side of the tone
unless you're the woman who stands every day
collecting columns of signatures in the mall,
the man we've been avoiding for weeks, the child
that rolled away and will not leave us alone.
If, on the other hand, this is a call
to tell us that you love us, give us a way
to be in touch again, the name of the bar,
maybe a number scribbled there on the wall,
the intersection nearest to where you are.
We've waited to hear you love us. It might not hurt
to know how much, but you don't have to say.
We probably couldn't handle it, anyway.
But bless your heart. Bless your heavy heart.

A QUESTION OF TIME

"Have you ever done this with another man?"
He liked to ask me that at random moments,
in little cafes, once on a ferris wheel.
I don't know why, a kind of game, I guess,
a way of being told what he had to hear.

I'd carried the word around for twelve years.
I was surprised to feel it coming out.
It should have lain there like the other times
but something in the question knocked it loose
and I was tired. We both should have been asleep.

I heard it coming as soon as I heard the question,
past my heart, through my throat, "Yes."
I felt a hollow place where the word had been.

He said, "I mean, since we've been married."
He couldn't let it go. I said, "Yes."
He looked from the sides of his eyes and saw I meant it.

He won't come back. I'd never ask him to.
First he was obsessed with the foolish question,
now he's obsessed with the answer. Still, I miss him.
I also miss the other man sometimes,
though I doubt that he could recall my name.

I let him do it because it made me feel good
to have somebody think that way about me.
It had nothing at all to do with him.

I got what I deserved. I did wrong.
But it was over so quickly, and it's been so long.

THE CURATOR

We thought it would come, we thought the Germans would come,
were almost certain they would. I was thirty-two,
the youngest assistant curator in the country.
I had some good ideas in those days.

Well, what we did was this. We had boxes
precisely built to every size of canvas.
We put the boxes in the basement and waited.

When word came that the Germans were coming in,
we got each painting put in the proper box
and out of Leningrad in less than a week.
They were stored somewhere in southern Russia.

But what we did, you see, besides the boxes
waiting in the basement, which was fine,
a grand idea, you'll agree, and it saved the art—
but what we did was leave the frames hanging,
so after the war it would be a simple thing
to put the paintings back where they belonged.

Nothing will seem surprised or sad again
compared to those imperious, vacant frames.

Well, the staff stayed on to clean the rubble
after the daily bombardments. We didn't dream—
You know it lasted nine hundred days.
Much of the roof was lost and snow would lie
sometimes a foot deep on this very floor,
but the walls stood firm and hardly a frame fell.

Here is the story, now, that I want to tell you.
Early one day, a dark December morning,
we came on three young soldiers waiting outside,
pacing and swinging their arms against the cold.
They told us this: in three homes far from here
all dreamed of one day coming to Leningrad
to see the Hermitage, as they supposed
every Soviet citizen dreamed of doing.
Now they had been sent to defend the city,
a turn of fortune the three could hardly believe.

I had to tell them there was nothing to see
but hundreds and hundreds of frames where the paintings had
    hung.

"Please, sir," one of them said, "let us see them."

And so we did. It didn't seem any stranger
than all of us being here in the first place,
inside such a building, strolling in snow.

We led them around most of the major rooms,
what they could take the time for, wall by wall.
Now and then we stopped and tried to tell them
part of what they would see if they saw the paintings.
I told them how those colors would come together,
described a brushstroke here, a dollop there,
mentioned a model and why she seemed to pout
and why this painter got the roses wrong.

The next day a dozen waited for us,
then thirty or more, gathered in twos and threes.
Each of us took a group in a different direction:
Castagno, Caravaggio, Brueghel, Cezanne, Matisse,
Orozco, Manet, DaVinci, Goya, Vermeer,
Picasso, Uccello, your Whistler, Wood, and Gropper.
We pointed to more details about the paintings,
I venture to say, than if we had had them there,
some unexpected use of line or light,
balance or movement, facing the cluster of faces
the same way we'd done it every morning
before the war, but then we didn't pay
so much attention to what we talked about.
People could see for themselves. As a matter of fact
we'd sometimes said our lines as if they were learned
out of a book, with hardly a look at the paintings.

But now the guide and the listeners paid attention
to everything—the simple differences
between the first and post impressionists,
romantic and heroic, shade and shadow.

Maybe this was a way to forget the war
a little while. Maybe more than that.
Whatever it was, the people continued to come.
It came to be called The Unseen Collection.

Here. Here is the story I want to tell you.

Slowly, blind people began to come.
A few at first then more of them every morning,
some led and some alone, some swaying a little.
They leaned and listened hard, they screwed their faces,
they seemed to shift their eyes, those that had them,
to see better what was being said.
And a cock of the head. My God, they paid attention.

After the siege was lifted and the Germans left
and the roof was fixed and the paintings were in their places,
the blind never came again. Not like before.
This seems strange, but what I think it was,
they couldn't see the paintings anymore.
They could still have listened, but the lectures became
a little matter-of-fact. What can I say?
Confluences come when they will and they go away.